I0590348

NORFOLK COAST
FROM THE AIR 2

DEDICATION

To the professionals and amateurs who over the centuries have striven,
sometimes successfully and sometimes not, to safeguard
this precious coast from the rages and ravages
of the North Sea, this book is dedicated.

NORFOLK COAST
FROM THE AIR 2

Mike Page & Pauline Young

HALSGROVE

First published in Great Britain in 2009

British Library Cataloguing-in-Publication Data
A CIP record for this title is available from the British Library

ISBN 978 1 84114 974 5

HALSGROVE
Halsgrove House,
Ryelands Industrial Estate,
Bagley Road, Wellington, Somerset TA21 9PZ
Tel: 01823 653777 Fax: 01823 216796
email: sales@halsgrove.com

Part of the Halsgrove group of companies
Information on all Halsgrove titles is available at: www.halsgrove.com

Printed and bound in India on behalf of JFDi Print Services Ltd

FOREWORD

Here is a further and unique set of brilliant aerial photographs that you will enjoy greatly. This time Mike Page has turned his interests in flying and photography once more to beautifully illustrate the Norfolk Coast as seen from the air. The coverage is comprehensive. From aerial views of The Wash to the west, around the coastline to its eastern boundary, including the newly constructed Great Yarmouth Outer Harbour.

Pauline Young's thoroughly researched accompanying text multiplies the pleasure of absorbing and enjoying these outstanding illustrations.

James Hoseason OBE
2009

ACKNOWLEDGEMENTS

We're grateful to the following for their help in the production of this second volume of aerial pictures of the Norfolk Coast:

Co-pilots Peter Day, Tim Ball, Brian Barr, Norwich Air Traffic and Richard Adderson, Dr Jenny Lawrence, Pat Lee, Jackie Routledge, Judy Speed, Ken Speller and, as always, our spouses Gillian Page and John Young.

Mike Page **Pauline Young**
Strumpshaw **Wymondham**

INTRODUCTION

Since our first book of aerial photographs of the Norfolk Coast was published in 2006 significant changes have taken place. Most striking perhaps is Great Yarmouth's Outer Harbour whose creation Mike has recorded from the start. Several pictures are included in this volume. On record also is the sea's continuing relentless attack on the more vulnerable parts of our coast, particularly at Happisburgh and Winterton. From the picture of low lying Horsey it's easy to see the effect that another great tidal surge such as that of 1953 would have upon the inland area lying beyond. We hope that you will enjoy this up to date record of one of the most beautiful and varied coastlines in the country.

Mike Page
Pauline Young
2009

Mike's cameras are a Canon 1D Mk2 digital with a 80-200 2.8 lens and a Canon 1D Mk3 digital with a 24-105 lens. His high wing two seat Cessna 150 aircraft is ideal for aerial photography.

All royalties from the sale of this book as with all our others will be donated to charity.

The Norfolk Coastline

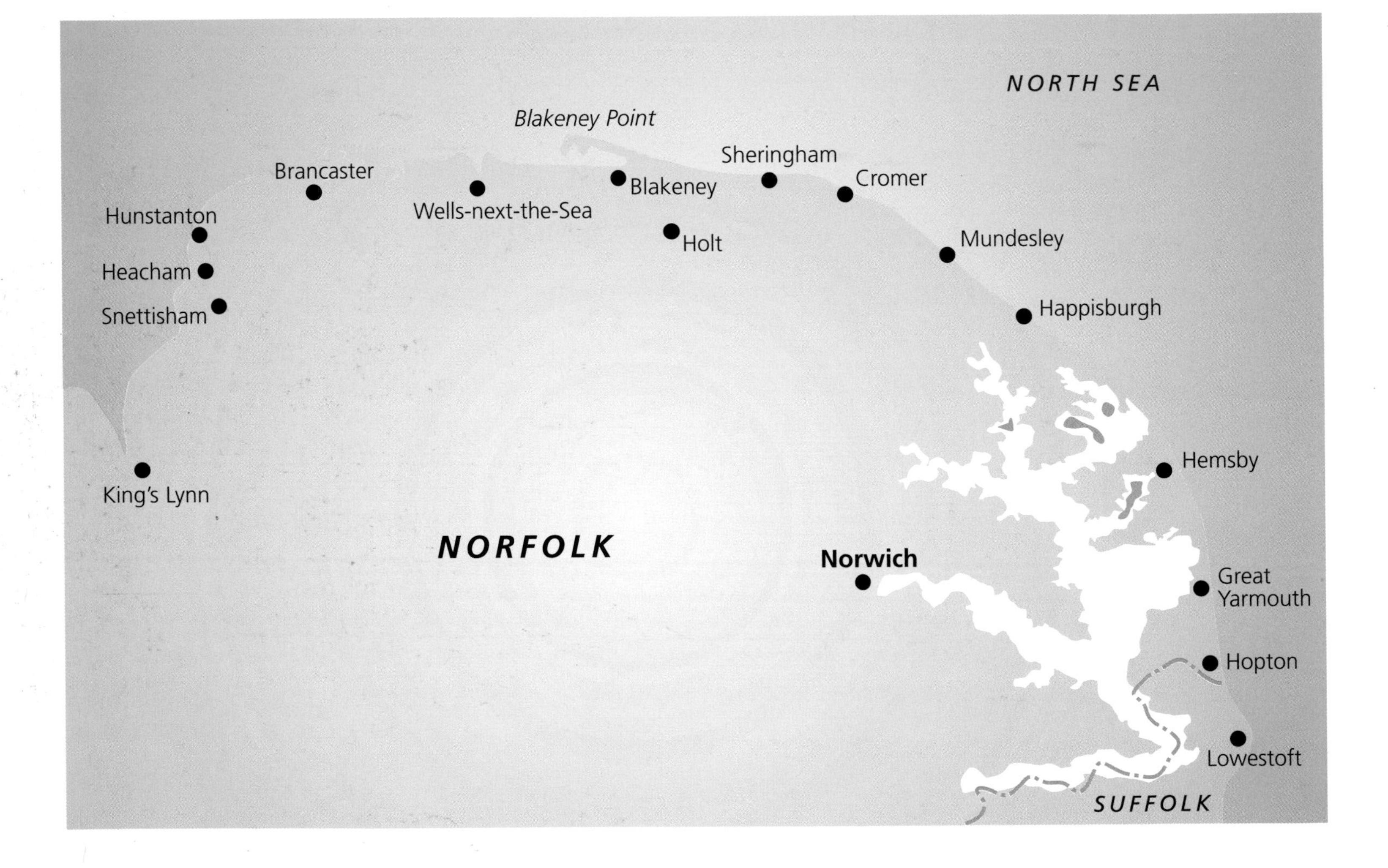

Hopton looking south.

Once a fishing village, Hopton is now both a dormitory village for Great Yarmouth and a holiday destination. Caravans and holiday camps occupy just about as many acres as does the permanent housing. And that's not the only identity crisis Hopton may have. With the reorganisation of the county boundaries the village previously in Suffolk, is now in Norfolk. Even the church has moved. Now a ruin, the original church was built close to the sea c.1090. In 1865 it burned down and was replaced by one further inland. A giant rusty anchor sits in the old churchyard, a reminder of the village's origins.

The promontory is Ness Point, the most easterly land in Britain.

A holiday with a view.
These holidaymakers from the caravan park are giving Mike Page and his aircraft an enthusiastic wave, little do they know they'll appear in this book!

Hopton looking north.
Only the golf course divides Hopton from Gorleston. The sand spit on which Great Yarmouth was built is on the skyline past Yarmouth's newly built Outer Harbour.

Gorleston Golf Course.

This is the first of several cliff- edge courses along the Norfolk coast, the others are at Cromer, Sheringham and Brancaster. It seems an extraordinary situation which wouldn't happen today but in 1914 the Golf Club persuaded the railway company to create Links Halt on the line which ran between Great Yarmouth and Lowestoft expressly to serve the golf club! The expanse of Breydon Water is in the background.

Gorleston beach looking south.
With the advent of the railways, holiday resorts became popular destinations and Gorleston's sandy beach was a great attraction. The town had no fewer than three stations – now it has none. The model yacht pond was created in 1926 as an unemployment project after WW1 and still is popular today. The site had been occupied previously by Parker's Donkey Stand giving rides on the beach for a penny. Lowestoft Ness is on the horizon.

Gorleston looking north-west.
Beyond the seaside buildings of Gorleston sea front stands the lighthouse (1877 and now disused) at Brush Bend. The name derives from the brushwood floated in on successive tides and used to consolidate the ground at the river wall.

Opposite: **Gorleston terraces.**
This is the area where the fishermen lived. Many men were employed on the drifters fishing for herring. During WW1 many of the drifters became mine sweepers and the men served on them as part of the Royal Naval Volunteer Reserve.

The narrow area between the River Yare and the Denes was the original town. Restrictions were imposed preventing any building outside it. This explains Yarmouth's famous Rows, 145 of them in lanes so narrow that from their upstairs' windows it was possible to shake hands with one's opposite neighbour.

Gorleston, Great Yarmouth and across Breydon to the marshes beyond.

The Outer Harbour, the sandy Denes, the river, the 'spending beach' at the right hand bend where disabled ships could beach and Yarmouth's quays.

Dry dock along Yarmouth's river.

Opposite: **Great Yarmouth outside the town walls.**
The expanse of Breydon Water lies behind the town. In pre-Roman times Breydon and the Halvergate marshes (right of picture) were part of a large estuary. Britannia Pier is lower left of picture and 'the waterways' lower right. These shallow channels are safe enough for children to drive small boats. The channels were dug and the site landscaped as another unemployment project after WW1.

Maritime Festival.
A replica of the 18th century frigate *Grand Turk*, an HM Customs vessel and a Norfolk wherry were all on display at the popular Maritime Festival when this picture was taken in 2007. *Grand Turk* featured in the 'Hornblower' TV series.

The Royal Naval Hospital was built around 1800 as a response to the Napoleonic threat. It later became part of the Naval Barracks whose Barrack Master in 1811 was Captain George Manby better known for his life-saving apparatus . Vice Admiral Nelson visited wounded soldiers there on his return from the Battle of Copenhagen (1801) saying to one young man who had lost his right arm "Why Jack, you and I both are spoiled for fishermen". (Nelson had lost *his* right arm at Santa Cruz 4 years earlier.) Two decades ago the listed building was skillfully converted to housing.

The Yarmouth Eye.
This latest attraction on Great Yarmouth's Pleasure Beach is a smaller copy of the London Eye. It operated during summer 2008/2009 being dismantled for the winter period.

Great Yarmouth's Outer Harbour, October 2007.

Before work could begin (2007) a sunken Dutch coaster which had been sitting on the sea bed since 1973 had to be removed. The £75 million project will have two breakwaters, each 1,400 metres long, and a 450-metre quay. Sand will be pumped from the sea bed to achieve a depth of 10 metres. Dredged sand is used to build up the new quays.

Great Yarmouth's Outer Harbour, May 2009.
The first ship to enter the new outer harbour. *Zhen Hua 6* delivers two container cranes, from China, to the dockside.

Above: **Scandinavian rock carried in by barge for the breakwaters.**

Right: **Placing the rocks in position.**

Sand is pumped from the sea bed.

Harbour piling, July 2008.

November 2008, getting there.

When one or two appear they're referred to as 'wind turbines', 30 of them become a wind farm.

Opposite: **Wind turbines on Scroby Sands close in to the shore.**

Caister beach looking towards Winterton Ness.
Caister was one of the many villages along this part of the Norfolk coast having a Beach Company. The companies, forerunners of the lifeboat service, went to the aid of vessels in distress once a salvage price had been agreed with the skipper. Caister today is proud to have an independent lifeboat supported entirely by voluntary contributions. Winterton Ness (middle distance) has over the centuries seen many shipwrecks on the treacherous sands in the shallow waters of the North Sea.

Caister village.
The Romans built a fortified town here. Now holiday properties and permanent homes surround the nucleus of fishermen's cottages whilst caravan parks begin what is a constant feature northwards along the coast as far as Sheringham.

Caister castle.

The castle's 98′ circular tower is more or less all that remains of a substantial fortified house. It was the first (1432) very large building in the area to be built of brick. The creator of Caister Castle, Sir John Fastolf, is thought to have been the inspiration for Shakespeare's Falstaff. The castle subsequently passed to the Paston family and is mentioned several times in the Paston letters which were composed by various members of the influential Paston family of Oxnead and Paston between 1420 and 1503. The letters, discovered in the eighteenth century, catalogue events both political and domestic and give rare insight into the times in which they were written.

Dune blaze.
Firefighters tackling a blaze on the dunes north of Caister. The dunes, besides providing wildlife habitats, are vital in helping prevent sand blow. Note the substantial sea defences.

California and the old railway line.
On the M&GN railway line from Yarmouth Beach Station to Melton Constable a makeshift Halt was created here at California in 1933, trains stopping there in the summer months only. The line, originally further from the water's edge, was closed in 1959 and the track taken up shortly afterwards. In the distance are the wind turbines of West Somerton.

Cliff erosion at California.
Cliff erosion is a problem all along the coast between Caister and Sheringham. The purpose of the line of boulders is to break the force of the waves before they erode the base of the cliffs. It seems the hamlet acquired its name from the discovery of a hoard of gold coins washed ashore probably from a sunken wreck and found at the base of the cliffs around the time of America's California Gold Rush (1845).

Scratby.
If erosion continues then in 20 years' time where will Scratby's cliff edge be?

Scratby August 2008.
The coastline is largely undefended apart from the boulders top left of picture.

Hemsby and Newport.
The holiday industry is very much in evidence. Winterton village and Winterton Ness are in the distance. More marram grass was planted after the devastating 1953 floods to stabilize the dunes. A map of 1754 shows Winterton Ness jutting out a distance of 1¾ miles from the village, today the Ness is hardly apparent.

Hemsby in the holiday season.
The West Somerton wind turbines are in the distance.

Winterton Ness.

There's a potential for sea incursion along the edge of the dunes mid-picture. Users have forged a path to give beach access for the houses and caravans nestling in the valley behind. But although the *coast* is at risk here, even greater risks and tragedies have taken place at *sea* off Winterton Ness. The sea has claimed possibly more lives and ships here than anywhere else along this stretch of coast. There have been horrendous shipwrecks. In 1554 for example in one storm alone 50 ships were wrecked off the Ness and many lives lost. It's not for nothing that sailors referred to the many sandbanks off the coast as 'The Devil's Throat'.

But from shipwrecks much useful building material has been washed ashore over the centuries. Writing of Winterton village in 1772 Daniel Defoe says:

> *There was not a shed nor a barn nor a stable, nay not the pales of their fences and yards, not a hogstye but what was made of planks, beams, whales and timbers – the wreck of ships and the ruin of merchants' and mariners' fortunes.*

Recycling is nothing new.

Winterton 1996.
Note the dunes on the seaward side of the car park.

Winterton 2008 dune erosion.

Winterton car park 2002

The blocks were put in place during WW2 to counter enemy tank invasion. Due to erosion over the years many blocks have fallen down the cliff.

Winterton car park 2008

The blocks have been repositioned in an attempt to protect the cliffs from being undermined by the force of the waves.

Winterton village.
The churchyard in common with Happisburgh churchyard bears witness to the tempestuous nature of the North Sea. Here there are graves of sailors drowned off the coast over several centuries. The high church tower as at Blakeney and Cromer provided a landmark for sailors.

Winterton and Horsey.
It's easy to imagine the devastation caused when the sea breaks through the dunes and floods the land behind. Horsey is one of the most vulnerable places along this coast. In past sea surges, the most recent being in 1953, salt water inundated the inland area with the result that hundreds of acres were ruined for agriculture for several years. In 1938 a tidal wave smashed through the sea defences causing a 700 yard breach and flooding 15 square miles. Sea defences were improved in the early 19th century by making the broad bank a uniform height as seen here. This in itself prevents all but the most severe batterings from a combination of gales and tidal waves.

The Horsey area is most at risk from sea surges.

The 1953 floods caused most devastation here at Horsey with thousands of acres under salt water. The picture shows a new rock groyne with older defences to the left. The groynes are placed at right angles to the dunes. Longshore drift is mitigated partly thereby retaining some of the sand and dune margin. The meandering former course of the River Thurne can be seen to the right of picture, the mouth of the river became blocked several centuries ago so its flow reversed. The Thurne today joins the River Bure abeam Thurne village.

Groyne building at Horsey October 2008.

Below: **Sand pumping at Waxham.**
Here at Waxham beach regeneration is taking place. Sand is dredged from the seabed several miles out to sea and carried inshore by the dredger. It is then pumped on to the existing beach thereby helping make good the deficit resulting from longshore drift.

GEOPOTES 15.
This high tech Dutch registered vessel of Van Oord is seen here pumping sand from its hopper onto the beach near Waxham.

Jet skiing at Sea Palling.
There's a Jet Ski Centre offering instruction in Sea Palling village.

Sea Palling reefs.
Mike Page shot this picture in February 2009. The reefs have been in place since 1995 as an Environment Agency funded Sea Defence and Beach Reclamation Scheme. There are 9 reefs, 4 are surface piercing breakwaters and the remaining 5 are breakwaters submerged at high tide.

Below: **Reef on a clear sea day.**
With water as clear as this on a summer's day it's no surprise that Sea Palling beach has been awarded Blue Flag status.

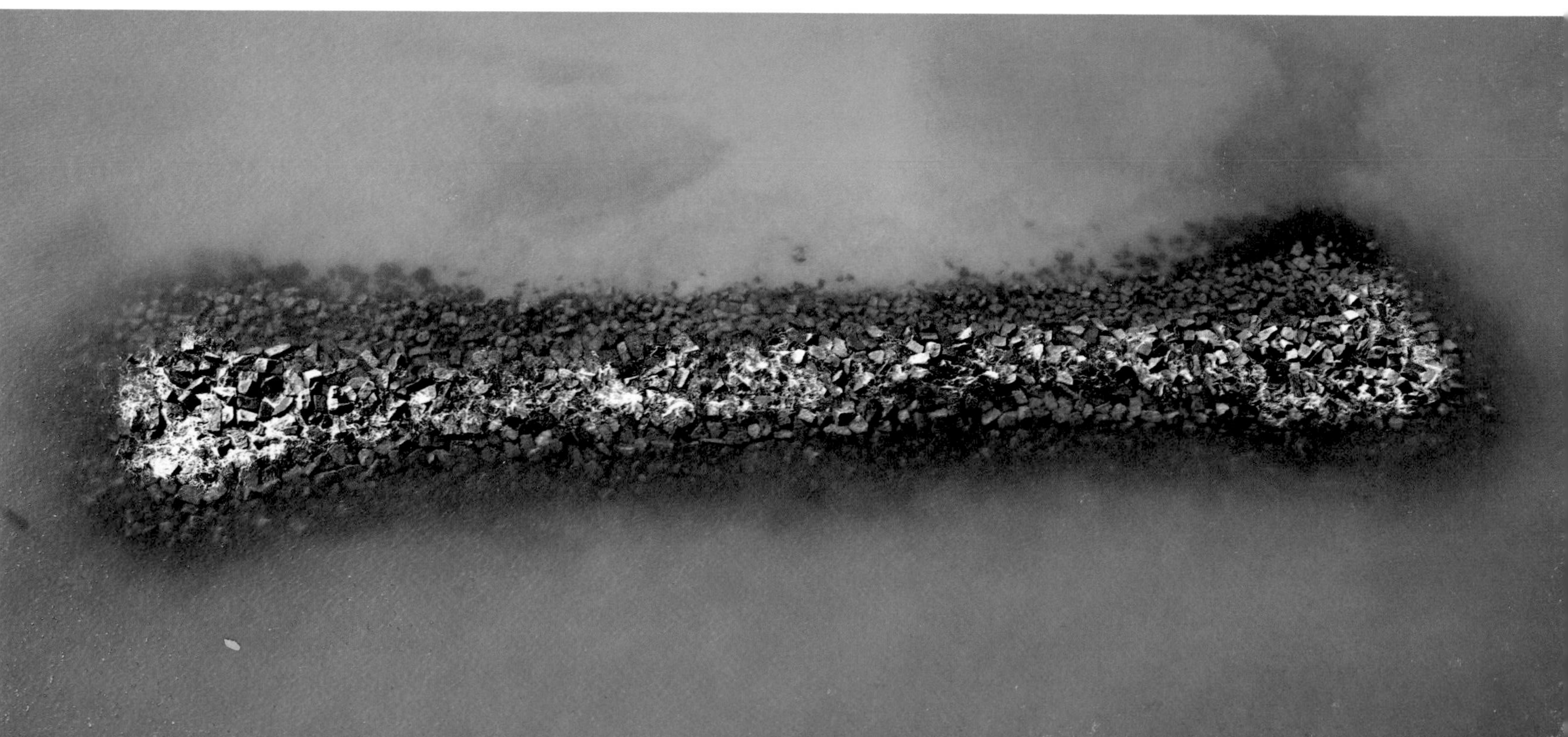

Sea Palling beach.
Sea Palling was devastated by the 1953 floods and 9 lives were lost. Since then a floodgate has been installed next to the inshore lifeboat station, a concrete sea wall has been built and there has been extensive planting of marram grass to hold the dunes.

Sea Palling village.

The reefs have given the village a 'breathing space' and only if the dunes were to be breached would flooding on a massive scale occur again. The church, unlike two others along this stretch of coast, is somewhat safeguarded by being set well back from the sea. The churches at adjacent Eccles and at Sidestrand have both crumbled down the cliff – almost in living memory.

Eccles.
All that is left of Eccles is the prewar Bush Estate – a collection of bungalows (some of them of timber construction) and caravans. The estate provides both holiday accomodation and permanent homes. But Eccles was once a thriving fishing town covering 2,000 acres. Sea 'rages' have been eroding the coastline here for centuries bringing the church closer and closer to the beach until in 1895 the last surviving part, the tower, fell into the sea. It was the third on the site so the Eccles name is appropriate – deriving from 'ecclesia' meaning 'church'. One far-sighted resident, William Laurod, in his will of 1597 required to be buried in the neighbouring inland churchyard of Hempstead. Although he couldn't know with any accuracy the fate of the diminishing coastline his fears proved him far sighted.

Eccles Cart Gap.
With its substantial concrete sea wall Eccles now houses Happisburgh's inshore lifeboat. Erosion damaged Happisburgh's beach ramp so preventing rescue launches by an all weather lifeboat.

Right: **Cart Gap's new ramp February 2009.**

Happisburgh. What's next?
After the houses have fallen into the sea will the wartime 'pillbox' be the next to go and after that the lighthouse?

February 1998.
A photograph taken by Mike Page.

Below: **February 2009**
Eleven years have passed since the previous picture was taken.

Property at risk, Happisburgh, January 2009.

Happisburgh Church.
Drownings off Happisburgh have been commonplace for several centuries; the evidence is in the churchyard. Thirty-two hands were lost from HMS *Poppy* whilst patrolling for smugglers in 1770. HMS *Invincible* a 74 gun Man-of-War was on her way from Great Yarmouth to the Baltic to join the fleet at the Battle of Copenhagen (1801) with 600 fighting men and a full load of provisions when she struck a sandbank on Hammond's Knoll and went down losing 400 hands; 119 of them are buried in the churchyard. Their memorial was erected in 1998. The last lifeboat based at Happisburgh was the 'Jacob and Rachel Valentine' (1907–26). It was sent by M&GN rail to Stalham then on by road. It took a team of 10 horses to launch.

October 2008, looking south.
It's a familiar pattern but where the revetments end erosion begins.

Ostende storm surge damage, November 2007.

Keswick and Bacton.
Keswick was once a small town with a flourishing sea trade. Now it depends mainly on the holiday industry and has a considerable number of retired residents. Mid-picture is the ruined Cluniac priory of Bromholme founded 1113. We'd know less about it had it not been for the claim that it possessed a piece of the True Cross (rood) so was a place of pilgrimage and mentioned both by Geoffrey Chaucer in *The Canterbury Tales* and in the *Tale of Piers Plowman*, both written in the 14th century. Bromholme flourished until Henry VIII dissolved the monasteries in 1535 after which it fell into disrepair.

Keswick and Walcott.

The villages of Keswick and Walcott adjoin. Coal and·malt used to be unloaded onto the beach and carried away by horse and cart from the Gaps but the railway killed off coastal trading. Both villages have been decimated by past sea incursions, concrete sea walls now protect what remains. The Beach Companies here were able to make a good living from shipwrecks. Mid-picture (right) stands what remains of Bromholme Priory.

Bacton Terminal.
New life was breathed into the area with the arrival of the North Sea Gas terminal at Bacton in 1968 with gas then harvested from the Leman field. Along with two other east coast terminals further north, 40% of the nation's power is generated by gas from the North Sea, distributed to UK customers via the National Grid.

Pipe laying.

A 295-mile long pipeline joins Bacton with gas fields in Holland and Belgium and, via a reverse flow Interconnector, gas can be transferred between the three countries as needed. The shallowness of the North Sea is a useful economic factor in gas retrieval, in recent geological terms England and the Continent were once one land mass.

Below: **Bacton, December 2008.**

Shell, Tullow, ENI, National Grid and Interconnector operate the terminal on five sites.

Mundesley.

The success of Mundesley as a holiday resort never quite came up to the expectations of those who built large hotels there in anticipation that the railway would bring in the visitors. Sadly for them the visitors preferred Cromer and Great Yarmouth. Nonetheless Mundesley is popular today and alternative uses have been found for the hotels and for the two sanitoria, which advertised the benefits of good clean Norfolk air especially for consumptive patients.

The 'golf ball' on the horizon houses radar detection equipment. Installed during WW2 (then minus the golf ball) it remains operational.

Stow Mill.

Standing by the side of the road out of Mundesley towards Trimingham the mill was built c. 1825, last used for grinding grain in 1930 and, appropriately, became the holiday home of a member of the McDougall's flour family. It was opened to the public for the first time in 1961 with new sails and a skeleton fantail. The present owners have hit upon a novel way to help cover the costs of the mill's upkeep. Fancy a model windmill in your garden? Here you can buy a concrete model of the real thing.

The Old English name for a resting place was 'stow' and it's thought that pilgrims on their way to Bromholm Priory rested here centuries before the mill was built.

Mundesley sea front.
Peaceful now but a memorial on the cliff top reminds us of the men who lost their lives in WW2 searching for and defusing bombs here. The memorial consists of the shell of a 500 kg German bomb donated by the Royal Engineers' Bomb Disposal Unit.

On the edge.
The occupants of the front row of caravans are certain of their holiday this year but will there be anything in which to stay next year? The revetments on the beach are only partially successful in breaking the force of the waves pounding the base of the cliffs.

The 'Golf ball'.
The landmark dome at RAF Trimingham houses surveillance radar equipment. Established in 1941 with the aim of detecting German E-boats and low flying enemy aircraft and transmitting the information to Mosquito Pathfinder bombers. It was closed for a while in the 1980s after the Cold War threat had abated but is now fully operational again. Today the greatest threat to the area is from cliff falls and erosion.

Trimingham village.
Here the soil comprising the cliffs is particularly crumbly and the only hope for the villages strung along this part of the coast road is to have adequate sea defences.

Trimingham, 30 September 2007.

Towards Sidestrand.
This picture was taken on the same day as the previous photograph, but further north.

Proof positive.

Compare the erosion of the cliffs with and without sea defences of revetments *and* groynes! The church (middle distance) is Sidestrand's second. The first fell into the sea. As one writer poignantly expressed the event:

> *"As the 'Big Push' (of WW1) was being formulated, the church tower slipped unwitnessed over the edge of the cliff and smashed onto the beach below". The Battle of the Somme took place later that same year. "Like the tower, a generation fell that was never to be".*

Village of millionaires.
Overstrand was another of the small fishing hamlets, which populated this coast originally but in the late nineteenth century it was dubbed the 'village of millionaires'. In the prosperous late Victorian and early Edwardian eras six wealthy people had homes there including Lord Battersea for whom Edwin Lutyens designed 'The Pleasaunce'.

Cromer Golf Course.
Lying between Cromer and Overstrand this is one of the Norfolk cliff top golf courses getting smaller as the cliffs crumble.

Cromer from the south-east.

Cromer's fortunes have been tied to the sea ever since it came to be on the coast – which wasn't always. Coastal erosion has taken its toll here as elsewhere over much of the Norfolk coast. Several centuries ago the village of Shipden bit by bit was washed away leaving only the ruins of the church. Church Rock is a hazard to Cromer fishermen at certain states of the tide. Cromer's most famous son is Coxswain Henry Blogg (1876–1954) the most highly decorated lifeboatman ever.

And Daniel Defoe (1660–1731) said of Cromer:

> *'Cromer is a market town close to the shores of this dangerous coast. I know nothing it is famous for (besides being the terror of sailors) except good lobsters are taken on the coast in great numbers.'*

Old Cromer.

The church tower is the highest in Norfolk (160 feet) and served as a landmark for centuries. In the absence of a harbour, rusty tractors pull fishing boats onto the beach where once colliers ran their boats aground to unload and barrow their coal at low tide. This picture was taken in October 2007 when the lifeboat on loan, the 'Royal Shipwright', was launched temporarily from the beach during alterations to the lifeboat shed at the end of the pier in readiness for the 'Lester', which came into service in 2008.

The cream painted Rocket House (left of the slipway) houses the Henry Blogg Museum and an excellent café. From the terrace on the opposite side of the slipway elegant Georgian houses look out over the North Sea

East Runton.
Crab boats waiting for calm seas on the slipway at East Runton.

How well do you sleep if your caravan is the one closest to the cliff?

Mammoth event.

In the cliff between East and West Runton in 1991 the skeleton of a prehistoric mammoth was uncovered. It's believed to have become trapped in the soft soil which today makes up the cliffs here. Its muddy grave would have been several miles inland at the time and part of the Cromer Forest Bed – a network of rivers and streams dating from before the first Ice Age 700,000 years ago.

West Runton slipway.

West Runton rock pools.
These West Runton rock pools are unique within Norfolk. Because of their chalk linings the pools hold the water even when the tide goes out so small fish, molluscs and sea anemones can be observed or caught to the delight of small children.

Beeston Bump.

The track across Beeston Bump is part of the Norfolk Long Distance Coast path, which terminates near Cromer. The hill is 63 metres high with a triangulation point at the summit. During WW2 the bump served as a Royal Navy 'Y' station secretly collecting and sending information to the Code and Cypher school at Bletchley Park; the concrete base of the installation is still there. The 'Y' station operated direction-finding equipment to locate some enemy transmissions and interpreted VHF radio signals from enemy E-Boats (fast surface vessels). And among the many alleged sightings of 'Black Shuck' is the rumour that the fierce black dog with red blazing eyes lived in the base of Beeston Bump. It's believed that Sir Arthur Conan Doyle heard about Black Shuck whilst staying at the Links Hotel, West Runton and created his story *The Hound of the Baskervilles* around the legend.

Sheringham.

The picture is of Lower Sheringham, which is the more recent of the two Sheringhams. Originally a hamlet of fishermen's cottages, it's now a holiday resort. The 'Poppy Line' railway, which runs between here and Holt, is a popular attraction and it's hoped that in the very near future this line and the commercial line from Norwich to Sheringham via Cromer (the 'Bittern Line') will be joined together. At present they're only a few yards apart in Sheringham town centre.

No harbour, just a slipway.

There's a splendid museum just off to the right of the picture. It contains the Henry Ramey Upcher rowed and sailed lifeboat, worth a trip to Sheringham just to see it. The museum will be moving, lifeboat and all, to an even better site along the seafront in the very near future and reinventing itself as a Heritage Centre.

Sheringham Wood in May.

The Poppy Line aka the North Norfolk Railway.
This volunteer-manned line has visiting steam and diesel engines on loan from different museums every year. The route between Sheringham and Holt is picturesque. The track runs part of its way alongside the coast with wonderful views of the Norfolk countryside.

Upper Sheringham and Sheringham Park.
Humphry Repton's favourite project was the hall and grounds of Sheringham Park (middle distance). It was built in the classical style and facing slightly east of south – Repton considered this orientation ideal. It turns its back to the sea and the cold east winds and lies nestled on the inland side of Oak Hill. Much of the woodland was already mature when Repton started on the park. He imported the rhododendrons and azaleas, which are a feature in early summer. Weybourne village lies in the distance with the Muckleburgh collection of tanks and army memorabilia beyond.

Opposite: **Upper Sheringham**
This was the original settlement (foreground) and although it lies inland is not entirely divorced from matters maritime; the mediaeval church has a mermaid carved on one of the bench ends.

Weybourne.
The most familiar fact known about Weybourne (apart from the knowledge that former PM John Major has a holiday home here) is the rhyme:

He who would England win
Must first at Weybourne Hope begin.

The beach slopes very steeply enabling ships (friend or foe) to anchor close to the shore. Certainly a watch has been kept at Weybourne in every war since. Elizabeth I ordered elaborate defences here against a Spanish invasion. There was a military presence during both World Wars with coastal guns in position. In WW2, an anti-aircraft practice firing range was set up. At neighbouring Muckleburgh a radar mast stands at the coast, it connects with masts at Trimingham and Hopton and is part of the country's surveillance network.

In 1858 an undersea cable was laid from Weybourne to Borkum, one of the Frisian islands in the North Sea.

Weybourne beach.

From Weybourne westwards the cliffs peter out until they appear again with a very different composition at Hunstanton. Smuggling was common all along the coast and here, for instance, in 1837 troopers waged a battle with smugglers and confiscated 240 gallons of brandy.

Kelling Heath.
Evidence of settlements dating from 6,500BC have been found here on Kelling Heath. The heath is historically a common. Two centuries or more ago the heath was used as a getaway route for smugglers and frequented by highwaymen (did the latter rob the former?)

Salthouse.

Light and airy Salthouse church, built in prosperous mediaeval times, is sited on the higher ground overlooking what was once the sea's edge. The village's descriptive place name originates from the salt produced here to service the fishing industry. Boats went out from all the Glaven ports as far as Iceland to catch cod and whiting. Then the harbour silted up, a familiar story along this stretch of coast. Landowners enclosed the marshes for grazing but the sea gets its own back every now and again and floods them extensively as in 1953. The shingle bank no longer maintained as a sea defence stretches 4 miles from Weybourne to Cley.

Bard Hill.
Bard Hill south of Salthouse contains a Bronze Age cemetery but was brought into the 20th century with a bump when a radar station (part of the Chain Home complex) was set up here. The station's purpose was to detect low flying (below 1500 ') aircraft and track German E-Boats. A Lancaster bomber crashed into the station's aerial in 1944 and although the aircraft managed to reach nearby RAF Langham the crew were killed in the crash landing.

The sea's revenge: November 2007.

Cley

Cley was once a flourishing trading port but marsh reclamation and silting up caused Cley's demise as a sea port. The coast from Salthouse to Hunstanton is a continuous nature reserve run by various conservation bodies including, as here, the Norfolk Wildlife Trust. Cley marshes are one of the most famous bird watching locations.

Cley Village.

In 1612 a fire gutted 117 houses at Cley so a new settlement was built closer to the coast and on the edge of the marshes. This left the church on the inland edge of the village. Smuggling was a widespread activity, the Custom Courthouse was built (1630) in an attempt to bring smugglers to justice. The famous landmark Cley Mill is situated on the western bank of the River Glaven; it was under 8 feet of water during the 1953 floods. Built in the 18th century to grind corn it now provides holiday accommodation.

Opposite: **Marsh patterns in the Glaven Valley.**

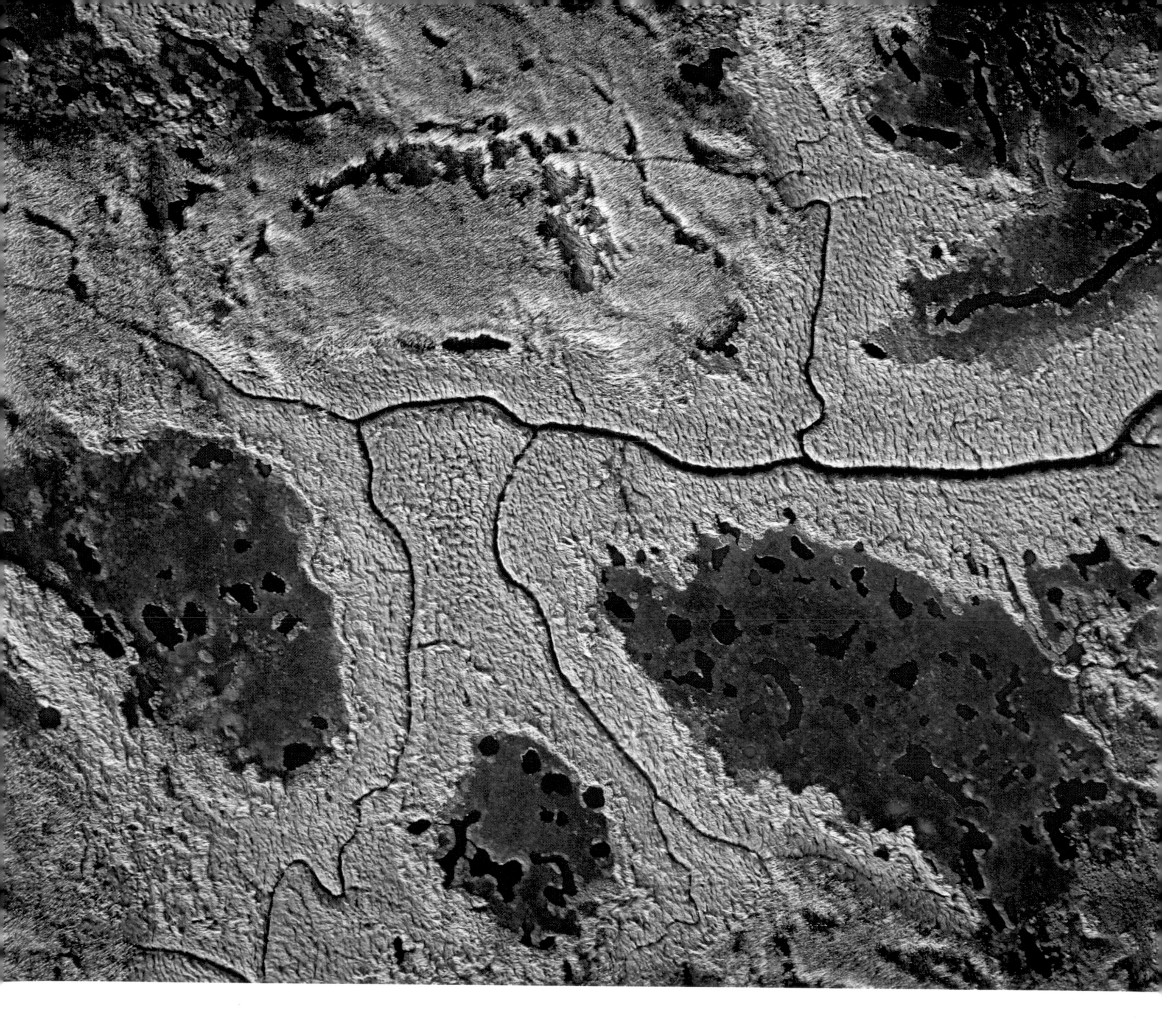

Cley reserve.
The pools and scrapes of the Norfolk Wildlife Trust's Cley marshes attract a huge variety of birds wintering, among them are brent geese, pintail and wigeon. Avocets, spoonbill and ringed plover are to be seen in the summer. But the year-round success has been the return of the bittern. Mike Page is fascinated by the patterns and colours of the marsh and particularly by seasonal change.
In the 17th century the shingle bank lay several hundred yards north of its present position.

Cley and Wiveton.
What is now tranquil marshland, with the River Glaven flowing through the middle and the villages of Wiveton and Cley on either side, was once a busy harbour! The gradual silting up of the harbour entrance and the enclosure of the marshes led to the decline and eventual end of sea-going trade.

Glandford

The River Glaven flowing through Glandford is one of the shortest Norfolk rivers. There has been a watermill here for hundreds of years, the present one dates from 1907. The ford from which the village takes its name was superseded by a picturesque mediaeval bridge nearer Wiveton, the bridge today carries rather more traffic than ever envisaged!

Blakeney Quay.
Blakeney's status has undergone considerable change over the centuries. In 1326 the harbour was so significant that it was one of only 50 in the country where the export of horses, gold and silver was permitted. When the Spanish Armada (1588) presented a real threat, 36 ships were sent from the Glaven ports of Cley, Wiveton and Blakeney. Up until the shingle bank began to build and the harbour silted up there was sea-going trade along the east coast and with countries across the North Sea. There was also a great deal of smuggling, in the 19th century it was known on the quiet that anyone with a horse and cart could earn a few shillings on certain nights by transporting barrels of brandy to secret destinations.

With so much seafaring activity it can be no coincidence that three admirals (Christopher Myngs, John Narborough and Cloudesley Shovell) came from the area with the most famous one of all, Horatio Nelson, born only a short sail and walk away).

Today Blakeney harbour is a paradise for small boats, holidaymakers and one of the two places from which to board a boat to watch seals basking on the sands of Blakeney Point.

Blakeney.
The curse of the meandering coast road (the A149) which bisects many of the villages between Wells and Cromer is somewhat mitigated by the historic and interesting places through which it winds, including Blakeney. Across the marshes stands Cley with its distinctive windmill. At its eastern end Blakeney church has a second tower where it's thought a light burned as a beacon for shipping.

Blakeney Point.

Low tide Blakeney Point.

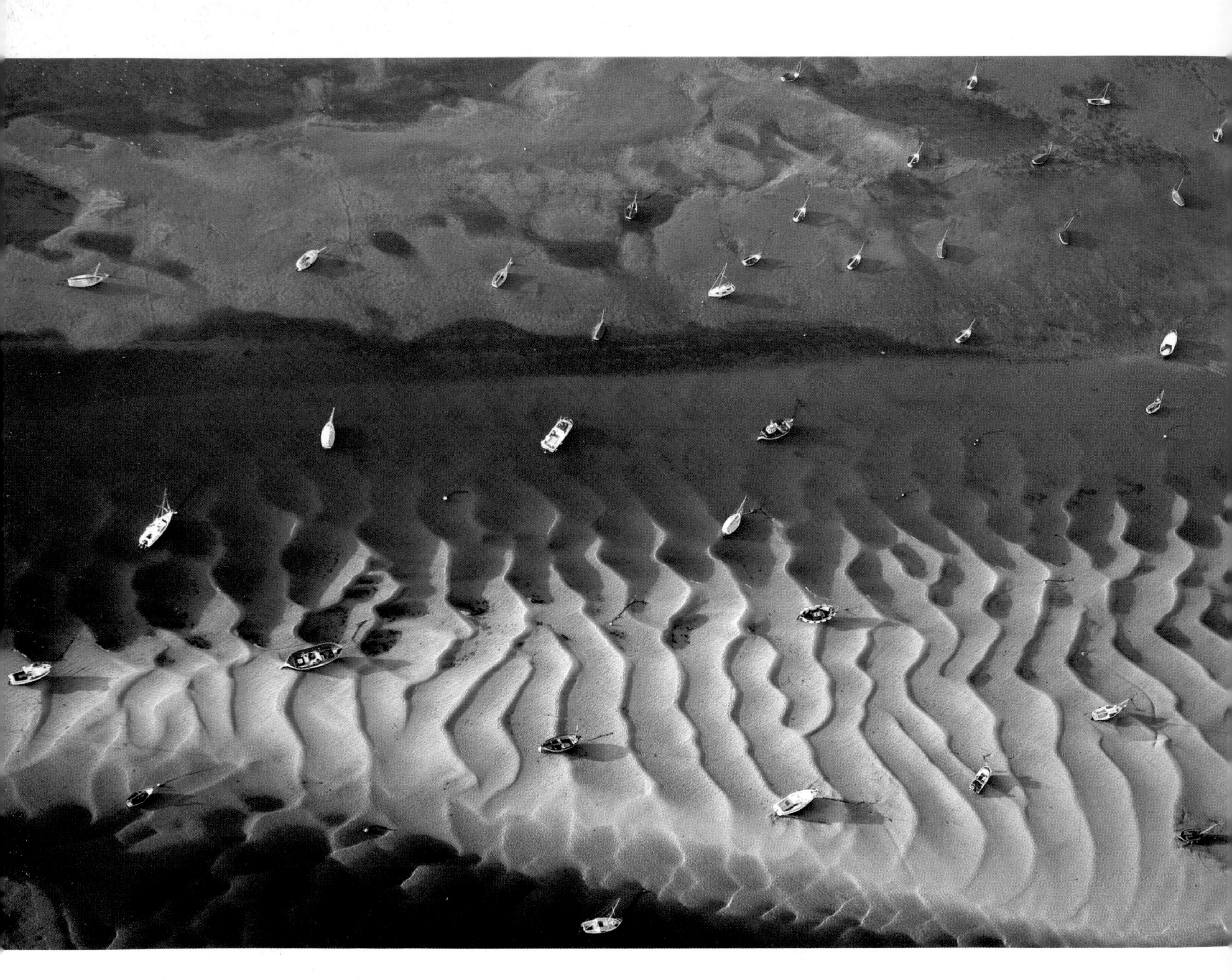

Low tide Blakeney harbour.

Blakeney Point looking across to Stiffkey marshes.

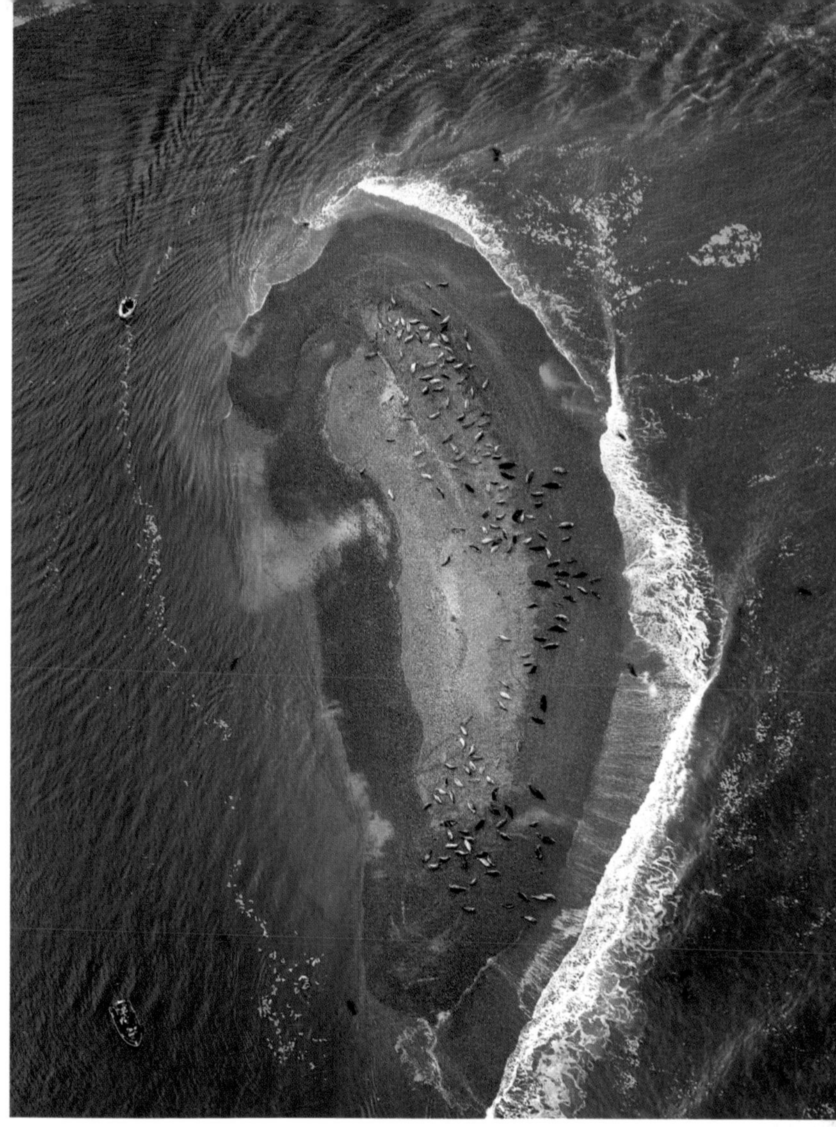

Blakeney seals.

Grey and common seals live on the sandbanks of Blakeney Point. The grey are the larger and have speckled coats, common seals have rounded faces and great big eyes. There are approximately 500 of them on the Point and as the average seal eats 10lbs of fish a day they're not always popular with the local fishermen. They *are* very popular however with the hundreds of people who each year are taken out by boat from Blakeney and Morston to see them basking on the sand.

Blakeney at sunset.

Morston looking south.

At high tide Blakeney harbour can be reached from Morston through a network of creeks. The National Trust owns the marshes on which samphire grows abundantly, it's a local delicacy but an acquired taste. During WW2 Langham airfield (middle distance) had Fairey Swordfish, Bristol Beaufighters, Wellington bombers and the B-17 Flying Fortress aircraft based there at various times. Many weary pilots after making the hazardous return flight across the North Sea were relieved to touch down here, their aircraft often badly damaged and barely able to stay in the air.

Today there's one aircraft engineer based on the airfield together with the inevitable turkey sheds which populate most disused Norfolk airfields. This engineer specialises in servicing Vintage aircraft and the biplanes which grace the skies complete a leisured picture with sailing boats below.

Morston Quay with Blakeney Point in the background.

Stiffkey saltmarsh.
The collection of Stewkey Blues (cockles) from the salt marshes used to be a job for the women of the village.

Stiffkey.
Stiffkey became national headlines with the unfrocking of its vicar the Reverend Harold Davidson in Norwich Cathedral in 1932 on the grounds of alleged immorality and association with Soho prostitutes. Next to the church is Stiffkey Hall. Built 1576 for Nicholas Bacon, Keeper of the Privy Seal to Elizabeth I, much of the building still stands and remains a private house. The River Stiffkey runs past the house to the west.

The fantastic patterns and colours of the salt marshes in July.

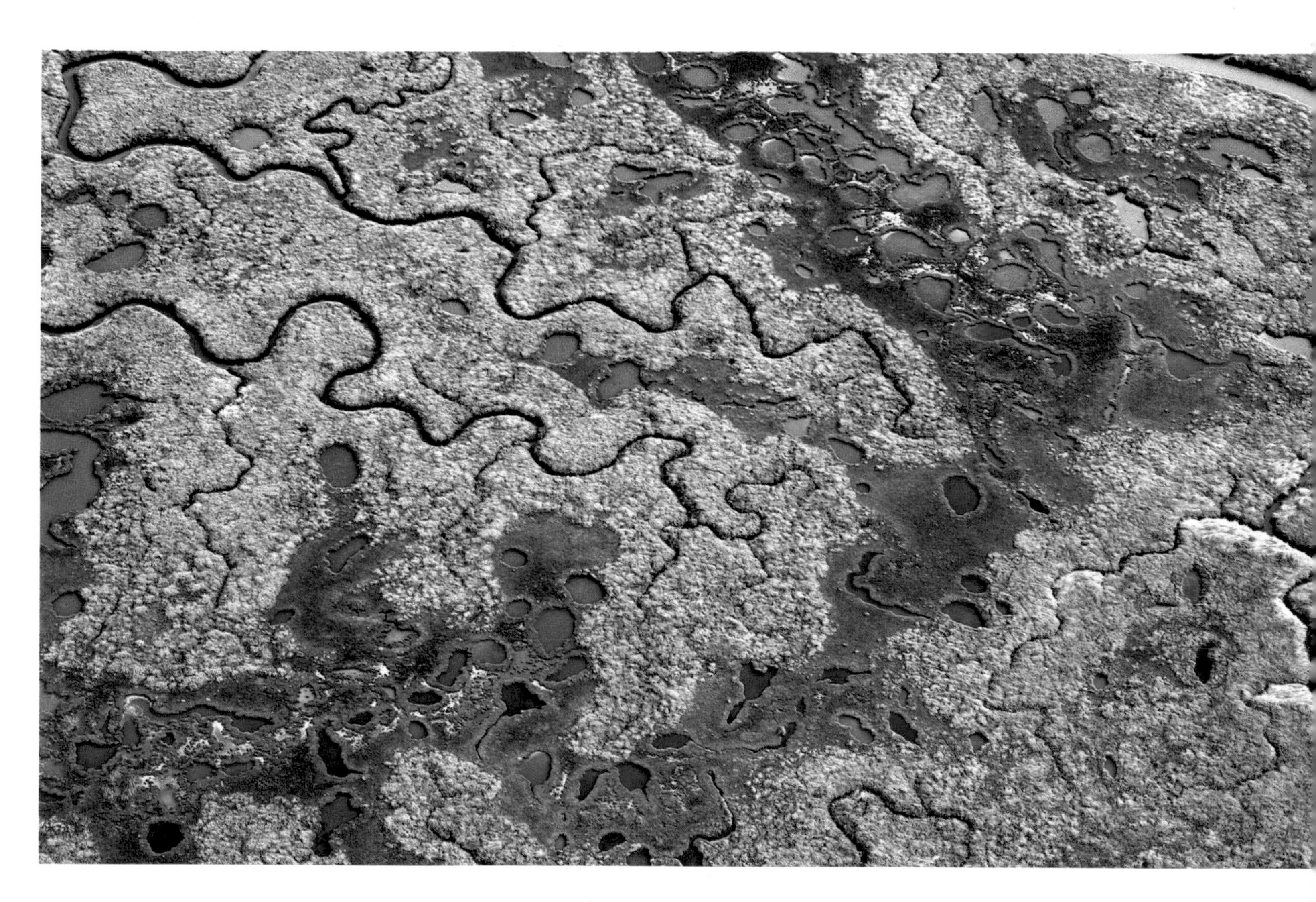

The same location in winter.

Wells-next-the-Sea.
Accurately described for the town is a mile away from open water. Once a busy sea-going town, today only leisure craft visit the harbour. Between the quay and the sea there's a stark contrast in appearance between the land to the right of picture and to the left. To the right lie East Hills and salt marshes, to the left is the land drained by the agricultural reformer, the second Earl of Leicester, Thomas Coke of Holkham in 1859. He created what was then possibly the best managed farming estate in Norfolk. The lifeboat shed is on the promontory and near to it is a boating lake which formerly (when there was sea access) was a haven for fishing boats. The magnificence of Holkham Beach lies beyond.

Wells harbour.

The harbour used to bustle with ships bringing in coal from the north of England and goods from the Continent. Grain and wool were the major exports. Now the large quayside granary has been converted to housing and the only large vessel to tie up here is the Dutch twin masted ketch *Albatros*, available for charter. The Harbourmaster's Office is to the left of the pontoon at which visiting sailing craft can moor. Across the road stands the sad memorial to the crew of the RNLI lifeboat *Eliza Adams* which capsized in 1880 drowning 11 of her 13 crew leaving 10 widows and 27 fatherless children. Wells features in the TV programme 'Kingdom' which, together with Swaffham, comprises the fictional town of 'Market Shipborough'.

High and dry in Wells at low tide.

Opposite: **East Hills.**
East Hills is in the foreground with Holkham Meals on the opposite side of the channel and the Holkham Estate's farmed land beyond. The Scots, Corsican and Maritime varieties of pines were planted to arrest sand blow and so enable the marshes to be drained for agriculture. These trees today provide a habitat for a wide range of birds including the crossbill which feasts on the pine seeds. Present too is the rare natterjack toad, recognized by the yellow stripe along its back.

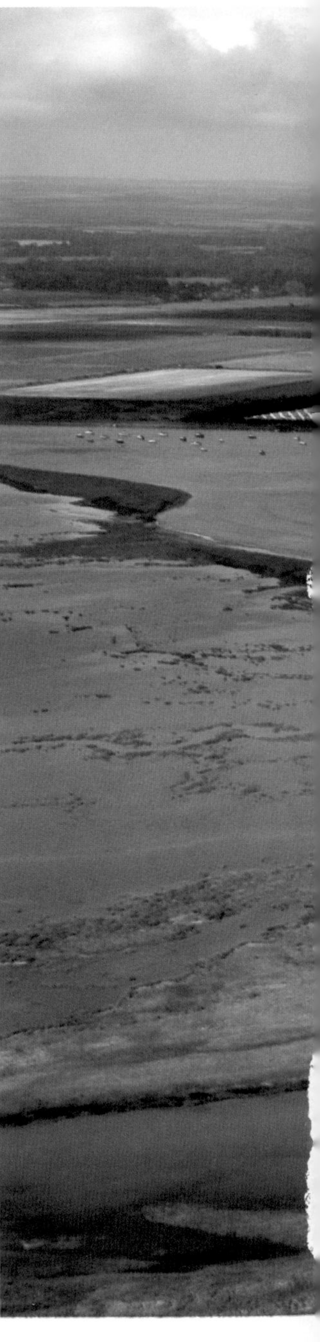

Wells harbour entrance.
To reach the harbour, boats have to circumnavigate one of the treacherous sandbanks which are part of the chain running along most of the Norfolk coast. These sandbanks have been responsible for the foundering of hundreds of ships over many decades. A pilot is available to guide craft into the harbour.

Opposite: **High tide at East Hills.**

Holkham beach.
Often described as 'the best beach in Norfolk' and arguably it is. The tide comes in very quickly so bathers and paddlers beware!

Holkham pines.
Caravans are numerous along the embanked side of the harbour channel but beyond, to the west, lie deserted beaches and wide Norfolk skies.

Holkham Hall.

Holkham Hall has been described as 'one of the two great Palladian mansions of Norfolk' (the other is Houghton). Built for the 1st Earl of Leicester by William Kent and Norwich architect Matthew Brettingham it remains privately owned but is open to the public. The ornamental lake was a salt water creek until the marshes were drained.

Holkham pines.
During May, June and July there are redirection notices on certain sections through the woods to steer walkers away from the colonies of nesting terns.

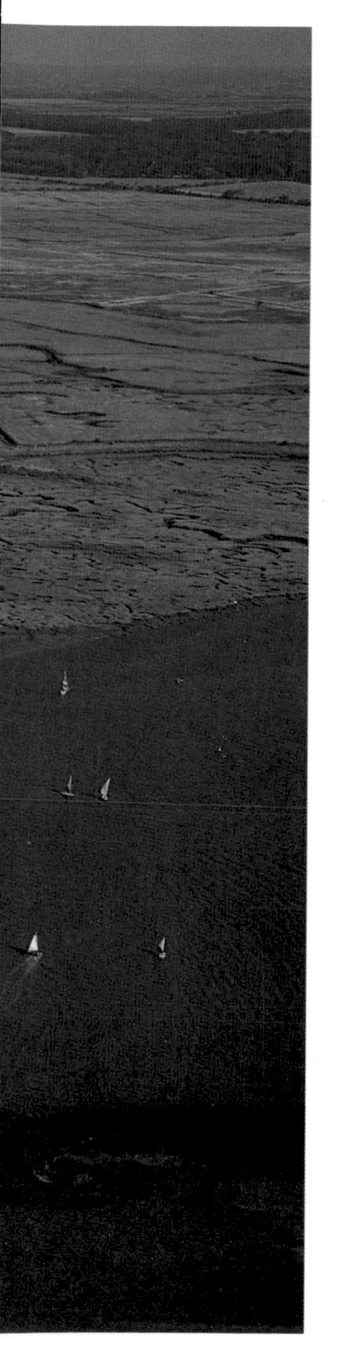

Burnham Overy Staithe.
This was yet another flourishing port until the railways came. Now it's heaven for small sailing boats. It's claimed that Nelson learned to sail here; appropriately the local pub is called 'The Hero'. In the summer a ferry operates across to Scolt Head Island nature reserve – a pass is required.

Opposite: **Overy Creek.**
The creek runs past Gun Hill (to the east) into Holkham Bay. Overy Marsh is to the left. The name Gun Hill harks back to the time when wildfowling was the main activity.

Burnham Overy.

The River Burn from which the Burnham villages take their name is to the left of picture. The A149 coast road runs past the mill and straight into the village. Oh for more by-passes!

Burnham Market.
During the Middle Ages it tended to be that one of a group of adjacent villages would become the commercial centre for the group as it was with Burnham Market. Because today of the high proportion of wealthy second home owners from the south, Burnham Market often has been dubbed 'Chelsea-on-Sea' but a kinder and funnier nomenclature might be 'Burnham Upmarket'!

Burnham Norton.
One of several Burnham villages within a couple of miles of one another. Another is Burnham Thorpe where at the time of his birth Nelson's father was Rector. The rectory no longer exists so the church has become the place of pilgrimage for Nelson devotees. In the distance lie Burnham Deepdale, Brancaster Staithe and Brancaster.

Brancaster Staithe.
Distinguishing it from the village of Brancaster 3 miles further west, Brancaster Staithe harks back to the time when trade came from the sea. 'Staithe' is Saxon meaning a landing place.

Brancaster Staithe, Mow Creek.
The most beautiful golf course and the western tip of Scolt Head Island.

Brancaster.
The Roman occupation of Britain had ended more or less by the end of the 5th century AD although their legacy of straight roads and place names and much more beside lives on. They departed from shore forts such as here at Brancaster although very little evidence of their buildings exists today because recycling is not a modern invention. The materials used in many local barns and pigsty construction bears this out. The fort stood on what is now the rectangular grass field next to the road on the eastern edge of the village.

The Royal West Norfolk Golf Club.
It is sited in what must be one of the most spectacular settings of any golf course anywhere. There's an unusual War Memorial in the form of two inscribed pillars, part of the entrance gate onto the course. The beach, along with all others on the east coast, was heavily fortified during WW2.

Brancaster harbour and the tip of Scolt Head Island.
Scolt Head Island is a paradise of mud flats and shingle, sand dunes and salt marsh where numerous birds such as Arctic and Sandwich terns and wintering wildfowl can be found. Miss Emma Turner, better known as an early Broadland bird photographer who lived in a houseboat on Hickling Broad, in 1924 wrote *Bird Watching on Scolt Head*. She became the Island's first unofficial 'watcher'.

Scolt Head looking west.
The Island's unusual name may derive from the appearance of some of its surface which is said to resemble ringworm on the scalp – 'scolt' may have been a local corruption of scalp.

Scolt Head looking east.

Scolt Head looking towards Blakeney with Brancaster saltmarsh and Mow Creek to the right

Titchwell.

In 2008 the RSPB which owns the Titchwell Reserve made the bold decision to allow the sea to encroach upon the salt marshes and to build a new sea wall behind the brackish marshes thereby protecting the freshwater marshes. This was done in order to prevent salt water inundation over the entire reserve. The brackish marsh will return to tidal salt marsh. The dynamics of this part of the coast, especially the gradual build up of the western edge of Scolt Head, means that in about 50 years' time Scolt Head will provide a barrier to protect the Titchwell Reserve. Avocets and bittern are among the rarer birds which now breed at Titchwell. The Reserve is open to the public year-round.

Titchwell looking east towards Scolt Head.

Thornham.

Fearing new ideas and damage to their fishing trade the 'rascally people of Thornham' in 1642 sabotaged the sea walls Dutch engineers were building. Distrust of 'furriners', i.e. anyone from outside the immediate area, was common.

Resulting from the Enclosure Act of 1786 many acres of salt marsh were embanked and became grazing land.

The Romans had a signal station here to communicate with garrisons across The Wash in Lincolnshire because of the ever present threat from Saxon raiders.

Thornham harbour.
After neighbouring Holme became entirely silted up (1827) Thornham benefited from Holme's lost trade. And even when the silting started to affect Thornham itself the channel was kept open to allow in 'billy boys' (coal-carrying barge-type boats) until just before WW1.

In an earlier century George Hogg built Thornham Hall (c.1788) with a rooftop lookout so he could watch for his boats bringing in their cargoes. He built 2 granaries, a jetty and a barn for storing ale from his London Brewhouse.

NWT Holme.
Where the North Sea meets the Wash at Holme the Norfolk Wildlife Trust has its Nature Reserve. The reserve is particularly noted for its migrant birds such as blue throats, it's also the seaward end of Peddars Way and the start of the Norfolk Coast Long Distance Footpath. In 1998 a timber circle of 55 oak posts surrounding an upturned oak tree were revealed on the beach. The circle has been dated to 2050 BC at which time the land would have extended a further 4 or 5 miles outwards. 'Seahenge' is thought to have been part of religious rituals during the Bronze Age. After a spell at the archaeological centre at Flag Fen, Peterborough the timbers are now on show at Lynn Museum.

Holme to Hunstanton.
As the coast turns west to face across The Wash, Hunstanton golf course (mid-picture) and the resort of New Hunstanton are both indicators of an area whose prosperity has become dependent on leisure pursuits. But the bright yellow flowers of oilseed rape and the green fields stretching into the distance are a reminder that Norfolk remains a predominantly agricultural county.

Hunstanton lighthouse.
What was known as 'the chapel light' because of its proximity to the ruined St Edmund's chapel of which only an arch remains, went out of service in 1921. It's now a private house. During WW1 it monitored transmissions from German ships and during WW2 it was an observation station and gunnery. The adjacent red-brick building is a voluntary lookout station used by the coastguard and when problems arise, the crew have pagers and get instructions from the Great Yarmouth coastguards. The paraglider is taking advantage of the updraught from the cliffs.

Opposite: **Hunstanton and The Wash.**
The LeStrange family of Hunstanton Hall (foreground with the original village of Hunstanton to the right) created the holiday resort of New Hunstanton often called simply 'Hunston'. The patronage of Queen Victoria's son, the Prince of Wales, helped to ensure the resort's success. The town was laid out by Victorian architect William Butterfield; local brown carrstone was used extensively. As Hunstanton's popularity grew a popular expedition was a boat trip across The Wash from Lincolnshire. The Skegness Steamboat Company operated paddle steamers departing Skegness 8am arriving at Hunstanton Pier 11am, cost 3 shillings. The pier, built 1870, was destroyed by a storm in 1978. Top left of picture is the entrance channel leading to Kings Lynn.

Hunstanton's cliffs.
The distinctive cliffs comprise clay at the base, carrstone in the middle and chalk at the top. The chalk seam runs as far as the Chilterns, many of the older buildings in Hunstanton are constructed of the carrstone giving them a brownish mellow appearance.

Hunstanton town.
Trains used to reach Hunstanton via Cambridge and Kings Lynn. To the railway went much of the popularity and prosperity of New Hunstanton. A supermarket stands on the former station site; the path of the rails which used to lead into the terminus is easy to pick out.

Kite surfing.
This is a popular pastime off the beach at Hunstanton and there's even a section for kite surfers within the local sailing club.

Heacham.
In the Middle Ages Heacham was a port. Where caravans now stand smugglers pulled their contraband from the beach to waiting carts. It's reckoned that over the Norfolk coast as a whole in the 18th century excise duty was paid on only a quarter of imported goods! Heacham's connection with Pocahontas' the Red Indian (or more politically correct American Indian) princess who married John Rolfe of Heacham Hall brought wider recognition to the village.

Snettisham Scalp.
The lakes were created from gravel extraction to build WW2 airfields. The Ordnance Survey map describes the wide expanse of Snettisham beach as 'Snettisham Scalp' which is curious. One possible explanation is that it relates to the beach areas where shell fish, cockles and, occasionally, mussels are found. In local dialect these areas are called 'scaups' - possibly a corruption of 'scalp'. Another Norfolk dialect word for scalp was 'scolt' as in Scolt Head.

The Ouse Estuary.
Snettisham and the mud flats at the mouth of the River Ouse. Here is an RSPB Reserve with hides and walks. A variety of wading birds populate the area.

Opposite: **Snettisham.**
Snettisham church spire is unusual, spires are uncommon in this part of the county although nearby Titchwell has a smaller wooden one. More noteworthy than Snettisham's spire is the Snettisham Treasure – buried torcs and other items of precious metal, considered to be the most important finds in the country and discovered in a field in 1948. Dating from around 70 BC and thought to be the royal treasure of the Iceni tribe the items are now deposited in the British Museum and Norwich's Castle Museum.

Kings Lynn.

The historic area of Kings Lynn lies mainly adjacent to the River Ouse where the elegant Custom House (1683) stands. It was built as a Merchants' Exchange but bought by the Crown in 1715. Trading has been carried on at least since the 1250s when the king's tailor imported the fur of the Arctic squirrel for HM's robes. Among Lynn's famous sons is sailor and explorer George Vancouver after whom the Canadian province and city are named. A cholera epidemic in 1897 brought rapid improvements in the town's water supply and required the covering over of most of the Millfleet next to the Custom House.

The 1960s town centre development has changed the character of the town.

Kings Lynn and the River Ouse.
The tidal River Ouse – at this point known as the Lynn Channel – was once narrow, winding and dangerous but has been widened and straightened as befits a commercial port. The river carries water from the complex drainage system of The Fens. A pilot still guides ships between the docks and The Wash.

Kings Lynn Docks.
Industry is centred round the river and the Alexandra (1869) and Bentinck (1883) docks. Kings Lynn is now the only commercially viable harbour between Great Yarmouth and the Humber Estuary.

When whaling was an important local enterprise the stench of blubber being rendered down made the town almost uninhabitable!

BIBLIOGRAPHY

Dymond David *The Norfolk Landscape* Alastair Press 1990
Harrod Wilhemine *The Norfolk Guide* Alastair Press 1958
Malster Robert *Saved from the Sea* Terence Dalton 1974
Meeres Frank *A History of Great Yarmouth* Phillimore 2007
Paston Letters ed Davis OUP 1963
Pevsner Nikolaus *North East Norfolk and Norwich* Penguin 1962
Pevsner Nikolaus *North West and South Norfolk* Penguin 1962
Pocock Tom *Pimlico County History* Norfolk 1995
Robinson Bruce *The Peddars Way and Norfolk Coast Path* HMSO 1986
Robinson Bruce and Mike *Walking the Long Distance Coast Path* Poppyland 2006
Storey Neil *The Lost Coast of Norfolk* Sutton 2008
Wade Martins Susanna *A History of Norfolk* Phillimore 1984
Williamson Tom *England's Landscape East Anglia* English Heritage 2006